The Sacramentals *of the* Church

By REV. LAWRENCE G. LOV

NIHIL OBSTAT: Daniel V. Flynn, J.C.D., *Censor Librorum*

IMPRIMATUR: Joseph T. O'Keefe, *Vicar General, Archdiocese of New York*

Through His Church Jesus teaches us and helps us to become holy through the Seven Sacraments and many Sacramentals.

SACRAMENTALS

SACRAMENTALS are holy things or actions which the Church uses to obtain for us from God, through her prayers, favors for our body and soul.

Sacramentals are like Sacraments, but there is a difference: A **Sacrament** is a sign that we can see, instituted by Christ to give grace. The Sacraments receive their power to give grace from God, through the merits of Jesus Christ.

There are seven Sacraments: Baptism, Confirmation, Holy Eucharist, Penance, Anointing of the Sick, Holy Orders, and Matrimony.

The **Sacramentals** were instituted by the Church and obtain graces for us by helping us to practice acts of virtue which draw down God's graces on us.

The Sacramentals obtain favors from God through the prayers of the Church offered for those who make use of them, and through the devotion they inspire.

Sacramentals do not give sanctifying grace but make us ready to receive it. Sacramentals prepare our souls to receive whatever grace God wishes to give us.

The Holy Trinity—Father, Son, and Holy Spirit—one true God in three Persons, lives in our soul by grace. Sacramentals prepare us to receive that grace from God.

HOW SACRAMENTALS HELP US

1. Sacramentals prepare us to receive *actual graces*.

Actual grace is a help given to us by God to offer light to our mind and strength to our will that we may do good and avoid evil.

"Sacramental" means "something like a Sacrament." Sacramentals do not of themselves give grace. Rather, they make us ready to receive grace by arousing in us feelings of faith and love.

2. Sacramentals help us to receive *forgiveness of our venial sins,* which are less serious offenses against the law of God.

3. Sacramentals obtain for us the *forgiveness of the punishment* we deserve for our sins.

4. Sacramentals obtain for us *health of body and other blessings* that we need in our daily life.

5. Sacramentals *protect us* from the power of the devil and temptations to do evil.

Jesus lives in us by His grace and helps us to live in Him by giving us the Sacramentals. They prepare us to receive blessings for soul and body.

THE KINDS OF SACRAMENTALS

The kinds of sacramentals are:
first, blessings given by priests and bishops;
second, prayers against evil spirits, called exorcisms;
third, blessed objects of devotion.

BLESSINGS

IN her blessings the Church shows how much she values the things of this world, which are God's gifts to us.

A blessing is a ritual ceremony by which a priest makes persons or things holy for divine service, or calls down the favor of God on what he blesses. The Church's ritual has over two hundred such blessings.

There are *blessings* for fields and gardens, cattle and schools, cars, houses, wine, water, fire and vegetables. All manner of persons and things are blessed.

Since the coming of the Son of God among us, all the world is consecrated to God's service. The Sacramentals extend Christ's presence to every part of our daily life. Things are blessed not only to ask God's protection on their use, but also to remind us that the life of Christians is to consecrate all that they use to the glory of God.

Karen and Tommy pray silently with their parents as Father John blesses the family car.

BLESSING OF THROATS

ST. Blase, Bishop of Sebaste, was beheaded after terrible torments in 317. Among his miracles is one in which he cured a boy who was choking from a fishbone. So he is venerated as the patron saint against diseases of the throat.

When the priest blesses throats on his feast-day, February 3, holding a candle and making the sign of the cross, he says, "Through the intercession of Saint Blase, Bishop and Martyr, may you be protected from all diseases of the throat and every other evil."

Mary, Joan, Pat, and Tony have their throats blessed.

Brigid and Timmy follow Father Andrew as he blesses a room of their home.

THE BLESSING OF A HOME

THERE is a custom of blessing homes during the Christmas Season especially among the German and Slavic people. This blessing is usually given by the pastor. He sprinkles the rooms with holy water and incenses them, then recites the prayers.

Exorcism is a prayer in which the priest commands the devil to leave a possessed person or forbids him to harm someone.

ACTIONS

MOST of the Sacramentals are *sacred actions, words, and objects*, to which the Church gives a blessing or by which she teaches the people that they can obtain certain graces from God.

Sacramental actions are movements of the body that the Church uses when honoring the Holy Eucharist and giving the Sacraments. Some of them are: kneeling, folding one's hands, making the sign of the cross, and bowing.

Kathy, Linda, Bobby, and Johnny kneel in prayer before an outdoor statue of Jesus on the Cross.

Children make the sign of the cross at the start of a new school day.

THE SIGN OF THE CROSS

WE usually begin and end our prayers with the sign of the cross. It expresses two important mysteries of the Christian religion: the Blessed Trinity and the Redemption.

When we say "in the name," we express the truth that there is only one God. When we say "of the Father, and of the Son, and of the Holy Spirit," we express the truth that there are three distinct Persons in God. When we make the form of the cross on ourselves, we express the truth that the Son of God, made man, redeemed us by His death on the cross.

Anna and Ralph make the Way of the Cross by going from station to station in the church.

THE WAY OF THE CROSS

THE heart of salvation is that Jesus Christ entered the glory of Resurrection through His suffering, Death and burial. Every Mass is the best Way of the Cross a Christian can share.

But piety inspired the Church of Jerusalem to celebrate the Mass at the very places where the scenes of the Passion of Christ happened, from the trial of Jesus to the grave. There are fourteen stations of the Cross.

1. **Jesus is condemned to death.**
2. **Jesus takes up His cross.**
3. **Jesus falls the first time.**
4. **Jesus meets His afflicted Mother.**
5. **Simon of Cyrene helps Jesus carry His cross.**
6. **Veronica wipes the face of Jesus.**
7. **Jesus falls a second time.**
8. **Jesus meets the women of Jerusalem.**
9. **Jesus falls a third time.**
10. **Jesus is stripped of His garments.**
11. **Jesus is nailed to the cross.**
12. **Jesus dies on the cross.**
13. **Jesus is laid in the arms of His Mother.**
14. **Jesus is laid in the tomb.**

BLESSED OBJECTS

SACRED objects are Sacramentals because the Church has performed a special blessing on them. A blessed object can mean a person, a building, and various things.

Some blessed *objects of devotion* are: holy water, candles, ashes, palms, incense, crucifixes, medals, rosaries, scapulars, images of Jesus, Mary, and the Saints, the clothing worn by men and women religious, the vestments worn by the priest at the altar, rings exchanged by a couple at marriage, the Bible and prayerbooks.

Father Vincent puts on the blessed vestments for Mass.

Clare dips her finger in holy water and prepares to make the sign of the cross before entering church.

HOLY WATER

WATER is a symbol of purity of body and soul. It is used in the ceremony of baptism, to show the cleansing from sin.

Before entering and leaving a church we bless ourselves with holy water as we make an act of faith in the Holy Trinity and thank Our Lord for having died on the cross for our redemption.

Sprinkling with holy water is done before the solemn Mass on Sunday and during the Mass on special occasions, such as weddings, funerals, and blessings.

CANDLES

THE candle is a Sacramental used in the Church's Liturgy. Candles were first used to give light in early morning services. They are an emblem of God, giver of life and enlightenment. Being pure, they remind us of Christ's spotless body, the flame signifying His Divine Nature.

Candles are required at the public administration of the Sacraments, at Mass and Benediction, at funerals and at other church ceremonies.

Candles burn brightly on the altar at Mass.

Philip and Ned light vigil lights at a shrine of the Sacred Heart of Jesus.

Candles are blessed on the feast of the Presentation of the Lord, February 2. They remind us of the words of holy Simeon concerning Christ: "A light of revelation to the Gentiles."

A procession of the people with lighted candles is held to remind us of the entry of Christ, the Light of the World, into the temple of Jerusalem.

The lighting of *vigil lights* is but a symbol of a person's devotion and a means of making an offering to the church.

THE CRUCIFIX, RELICS, AND SACRED IMAGES

W E honor Christ and the Saints when we pray before the crucifix, relics, and sacred images because we honor the persons they represent. We adore Christ, but we venerate the Saints and Our Lady.

When we pray to the Saints we ask them to offer their prayers to God for us because they are with God and have great love for us.

Before their soccer game, a team of boys from St. Aloysius School prays by an outdoor statue of the Saint.

Deacon Ray incenses the Book of Gospels before proclaiming the Gospel at Mass.

INCENSE

INCENSE is an aromatic gum in the form of powder or grains that give off a fragrant smoke when they are burned. When blessed it is a Sacramental. Its burning means zeal; its fragrance, virtue; its rising smoke, our prayer going to God.

It is used at Mass, for the Gospel book, the altar, the people and ministers, and the bread and wine; before consecration; at benediction of the Blessed Sacrament; during processions; at funerals.

Boys and girls receive ashes from Father Louis on Ash Wednesday.

ASHES

WHEN blessing and giving ashes on Ash Wednesday, the priest says, "Lord bless the sinner who asks for your forgiveness and bless all those who receive these ashes. May they keep this lenten season in preparation for the joy of Easter."

Ashes are used as the mark of our repentance. When the priest places ashes on those who come forward, he says to each one: "Turn away from sin and be faithful to the gospel." Or "Remember, man, you are dust and to dust you will return."

PALMS

ON Palm Sunday, when the priest blesses the palm branches, he says, "Almighty God, we pray, bless these branches and make them holy. Today we joyfully acclaim Jesus our Messiah and King. May we reach one day the happiness of the new and everlasting Jerusalem by faithfully following Him. May we honor You every day by living always in Him for He is Lord for ever."

By using blessed palms we also ask God to protect and help us.

Connie and Angela leave Mass on Palm Sunday, holding their palm branches.

HOLY OILS

HOLY oil stands for strength, sweetness, and spiritual activity. Christians are sometimes called "athletes of Christ," and so they are anointed with holy oil in order to remain spiritually strong.

Holy oil symbolizes Christ's priestly and kingly power in which all who are baptized share—His royal priesthood. It also symbolizes the imparting of the grace of the Holy Spirit.

The Church uses three types of holy oil: (1) "Oil of the Catechumens" at Baptism and Holy Orders; (2) "Holy Chrism" at Baptism, Confirmation, and Episcopal Ordinations; and (3) "Oil of the Sick" at the Anointing of the Sick.

WORDS

WORDS, too, can be sacred. They become Sacramentals when what is said has been made holy by the Church. Such words are *indulgenced prayers*. An indulgence is the forgiveness granted by the Church of the punishment which we deserve for the sins already forgiven.

At noon Carl and Carmela stand in the open fields and say an indulgenced prayer to Mary: the Angelus.

THE ROSARY

THE Rosary is a devotional prayer honoring the Mother of God. It is said on a string of beads made up of five sets each of one large and ten smaller beads, called decades. On the large beads the Our Father is said; on the small ones, the Hail Mary.

While saying twenty decades, we think about the joyous, luminous, sorrowful, or glorious parts of Our Lord and Our Lady's life, called the Mysteries of the Rosary.

At Lourdes, France, in 1858, the Blessed Virgin appeared to Bernadette and said the Rosary with her. At Fatima, Portugal, in 1917, she said the Rosary with the three children to whom she appeared, and said, "I am the Lady of the Rosary, and I have come to warn the faithful to amend their lives and ask pardon for their sins. People must not continue to offend the Lord, who is already so deeply offended. They must say the Rosary."

The Rosary is a Sacramental. The Rosary is a devotion most pleasing to our Blessed Mother and to Our Lord, because during the recitation of the Our Father and Hail Mary we think about their lives and the love they showed for us.

THE MYSTERIES OF THE ROSARY

THE JOYFUL MYSTERIES

1. The Annunciation
2. The Visitation
3. The Nativity
4. The Presentation in the Temple
5. Finding of the Child Jesus in the Temple

THE LUMINOUS MYSTERIES

1. Christ's Baptism
2. The Wedding at Cana
3. Proclamation of the Kingdom
4. The Transfiguration
5. Institution of the Eucharist

THE SORROWFUL MYSTERIES

1. The Agony in the Garden
2. The Scourging
3. The Crowning with Thorns
4. The Carrying of the Cross
5. The Crucifixion

THE GLORIOUS MYSTERIES

1. The Resurrection
2. The Ascension
3. The Descent of the Holy Spirit
4. The Assumption
5. The Coronation of the Blessed Virgin

RELICS AND SCAPULARS

WE honor *relics* because they are the bodies of the Saints or objects connected with the Saints or with Our Lord.

The Church has also approved a number of blessed scapulars as two small pieces of cloth joined by strings and worn around the neck and under the clothes. The best known is the brown scapular of Our Lady of Mount Carmel.

The scapular medal is a blessed medal, worn or carried on the person, instead of one or more of the small scapulars. It bears on one side a picture of the Sacred Heart, and on the other an image of the Blessed Virgin Mary.

While Betty kisses the relic of St. Frances Cabrini, Jennie puts on her scapular.

Mark reads the Bible at his desk while Andy uses his prayerbook.

THE BIBLE AND PRAYERBOOKS

THE *Bible* is the Word of God. Inspired by the Holy Spirit it is the written story of God's actions in the world and the teachings of Jesus, His Son, and of His Apostles.

Prayerbooks are used to help us speak to God. We say prayers from a prayerbook or use our own words. Prayerbooks also teach us about God and His Church and her teachings.

A *Missal* is a prayerbook containing the prayers recited by the priest at Mass, the Scripture Readings that are proclaimed, and the parts that are to be recited by the people.

THE LITURGICAL YEAR

There are three cycles in the Church year according to the most important mysteries of Our Lord's life: Christmas, Easter, and Pentecost. All are called to share in the liturgical prayer of the Church. Liturgical seasons and feasts are Sacramentals given to us by the Church.

SACRED TIMES

THE *liturgical seasons, feasts, and fasts of the Church* are Sacramentals which are given to us by the Church to make our faith stronger and to prepare our souls to serve God more generously.

Seasons of the Church: In Advent we look forward to the coming of the Lord by remembering the prophecies that foretell His birth, and we look forward to His coming on the last day.

In the Christmas Season we think of the earthly birth of the Savior and also His childhood and hidden life at Nazareth.

During the Lenten Season we think about the Passion and Death of Jesus to help us carry our daily cross by following Him.

In the Easter Season we think of the Resurrection and Ascension of Christ, and the coming of the Holy Spirit at Pentecost.

In the series of weeks from Pentecost to Advent we think of our salvation by following Christ in His teaching and example.

Feastdays of the Saints: The feasts of the Saints proclaim the wonderful works of Christ in His servants, and offer us examples to imitate.

Pilgrims come from all over the world to visit the shrine of Our Lady of Lourdes.

SACRED PLACES

BESIDES sacred times, there are sacred places. These places are set aside for Divine Worship. This means God is there in a presence that is more grace-filled than His usual presence in creation.

All churches are sacred places. The activities that Catholics carry out in them will be more open than any other place to God's grace and beneficial to their own salvation and that of the world.

There are also many shrines in different parts of the world, where God grants special favors on those who come to pray there. Some of these shrines are: Lourdes, in France; Fatima in Portugal; Guadalupe in Mexico City; Assisi in Italy; St. Anne de Beaupré in Canada; Czestochowa in Poland; and the Holy Places in Palestine.

In some countries, the shrines become national symbols of the devotion of the people, in which they show their deep faith in God, Our Lady, and the Saints.

Through Sacramentals we share in the life of Jesus.

FAITH IN THE USE OF SACRAMENTALS

SACRAMENTALS are not some kind of charm that works magically by just being had or worn or said. We must use the sacramentals with faith that they may help us as the Church wants them to help us.

This also calls for hope that what the Church encourages, Christ also blesses with His heavenly grace. For the Sacramentals carry with them the promise of God's help for soul and body, on the authority of the Church.

Using the Sacramentals should help us to serve God better.